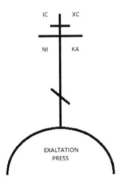

IC   XC

NI   KA

EXALTATION
PRESS

Approved for distribution by the Publishing Committee of the Russian Orthodox Church.

From the series "Scripture and Feasts for Children"

Elena Trostnikova

The Resurrection of Christ

Illustrations by Olga Podivilova

Translated by Fr. John Hogg

Copyright © 2019 Exaltation Press

Author: Elena Trostnikova
Illustrator: Olga Podivilova
Translator: Fr. John Hogg

"The Resurrection of Christ"
This book is part of the series "Scripture and Feasts for Children." It is about the Great Feast of the Nativity of Christ and is intended for reading to small children. The story here contained is structured close to the Gospel narrative, written in a simple and clear style for children with the addition of bright illustrations to help children understand as much as possible about the Savior's crucifixtion, death, burial, and resurrection.
The book also includes a guide for parents to help them talk to their children about Christ's passion, death, burial, and Resurrection.

Translated from the original "Воскресение Христово" by Nikea Press, Copyright © Trading house «NIKEA», www.Nikeabooks.ru

ISBN: 978-1-950067-03-9 (Paperback)

Edited by Cynthia Hogg

First printing edition 2019

Exaltation Press
Grand Rapids, MI

www.ExaltationPress.com

For bulk orders, please contact editor@exaltationpress.com.

TABLE OF CONTENTS

CHRIST IS RISEN!

Pascha is the greatest and most joyful feast. On this day, even the way we greet each other is different. Instead of saying "Hello!" we say "Christ is risen!" and answer "Truly He is risen!" and joyfully exchange the Paschal kiss. Everyone is kind, everyone is happy, as we exchange dyed eggs, have company over, and feast on Paschal foods, like kulich and cheese Pascha. Everything is delicious, everything is beautifully decorated. At Church, the bells ring out all day and all week. The feast is everywhere and in everything. But what exactly is this day? And why is it the most festive day of the year? And what do the words "Christ is risen" and "Truly He is risen" actually mean?

GOD LOVES US ALL

God created the world and all the people in it. We are all His children and He loves each of us. Many times, God showed mankind the path leading to eternal life but we were disobedient. Then He Himself became Man, was born (we celebrate His Nativity in the winter), grew, and lived among us and taught us to be kind and to love one another.

He also performed miracles. He healed the sick, gave sight to the blind, fed multitudes of people with a few small loaves of bread and two fish, and commanded a storm to stop, making the stormy seas calm. Then He walked on the water. He did all of this so that people would believe in Him and listen to Him.

CHRIST IS THE CONQUEROR OF DEATH

A few times, Christ even raised the dead, bringing them back to life. Once, he raised a boy who was being carried to be buried and another time he raised a young girl who had just died.

Later, He raised His friend Lazarus. Lazarus had died and was buried in a cave that was used as a tomb. The entrance into the cave was covered with a large stone.

The Lord came on the fourth day after Lazarus had died and said:

"Roll away the stone from the tomb!"

When they had rolled away the stone, he said:

"Lazarus, come forth!"

And Lazarus came out of the tomb, alive, resurrected!

There had never been anything like that before, anywhere! A man, dead and buried, coming back to life and coming out of the grave! When the people saw it, they realized that Jesus Christ is the Conqueror of death, that He is the Savior.

THE ENTRANCE OF THE LORD
INTO JERUSALEM

The Lord raised Lazarus from the dead at a time when many people had gathered in the holy city of Jerusalem from all corners of the Holy Land. They came because it was almost time to celebrate a great feast that they were supposed to celebrate in the temple in Jerusalem. And all of these people heard about the great miracle that had taken place, about how Lazarus had been raised from the dead. They all wanted to see the Savior, the Conqueror of death, with their own eyes and worship Him.

The Lord Jesus Christ said to His disciples:

"Go into Jerusalem. There you will find tied a donkey and

her colt. Bring that colt to Me."

And so they did. They spread out their clothes on the back of the donkey and the Lord sat on it and rode into Jerusalem.

As He rode, people came running from all directions, wanting to see Him. They cried, "The Savior is coming! The Conqueror of death, Who raised Lazarus! Blessed is He who comes in the name of the Lord. Hosanna!"

Many of them waved palm branches and threw them on the ground in front of the donkey. At the time, it was the custom to greet victorious leaders by waving palm branches. Some of them even spread out their robes on the road so that the Savior would ride over them on the donkey like on a carpet. Little boys climbed up the trees to see Him. There were so many people that not all of them could see Him. The little children rejoiced and cried, "Hosanna!" which means "Salvation!"

But there were also some in the crowd who were wicked and they hated godly people in the crowd for their goodness. These wicked people, the Pharisees[1], thought of themselves as teachers of the people and they wanted the people to listen to them, not to some other person. They wanted the people to cry out about them, "Look! Our saviors!"

Jesus Christ rode into Jerusalem on a donkey through the big gates in the stone wall that surrounded the city. The people who had met Him along the way ran after Him and cried, "Hosanna!" When the people in the city heard it, who still did not know what was happening, they asked who it was.

"It is Jesus, the Savior! It is the One who raised Lazarus!" they heard in reply. Then they, too, ran after Jesus and joyfully cried out "Hosanna! Hosanna! Our salvation is coming!"

The Pharisees were shaking with anger. They realized that all the people would follow Jesus and no one would listen to them anymore. "The whole world follows Him and we cannot do anything about it!" they said to each other.

---

1   Words written in red are explained in the glossary at the end of the book

PALM SUNDAY

One week before Pascha, the Church commemorates the Entrance of the Lord into Jerusalem. This feast is also called Palm Sunday. On Palm Sunday, we go out to meet Christ and rejoice like the children and adults once rejoiced. They went out with palm branches to greet the Conqueror of death. On this feast, we also carry palm branches. In the springtime, before the new leaves appear, pussy willow trees sprout beautiful, tiny, fluffy white blossoms on their branches. We can carry these branches too as we greet Christ. The palms and branches are blessed with holy water so they are no longer simple branches, but holy and festive.

THE MYSTICAL SUPPER

The wicked Pharisees hated the Lord so much that they decided to put Him to death. They were just waiting for the right opportunity to seize Him when there was no one to protect Him, since all the people loved Him. They had even promised to give money to whoever could help them capture Him.

One of the disciples of Christ, named Judas, was very greedy. He came to the Pharisees and said:

"How much money will you give me if I betray Him to you?"

They were very glad and promised to pay him a lot of money if he helped them capture Christ.

Jesus Christ knew about Judas's betrayal and that He would soon be captured and killed. He gathered together with His friends and disciples for the last time for supper. They had to meet in secret. This was the Mystical Supper.

When they were all at table, He took bread, broke it, and gave it to them, saying:

"This bread is My Body and when you eat it, I will be with you."

Then He took a cup with wine and said to them:

"This cup is My Blood. In it, I'm giving you Myself and when you drink from it, I will be with you."

And that is how Jesus Christ for the first time gave Communion

so that all who love Him could also receive Communion. Even today, He gives us Communion in His Body and Blood in Church so that, by receiving God, we can be united to Him.

The Lord Jesus Christ told His disciples that wicked people would kill Him and that on the third day, He would be resurrected, that is, rise from the dead. But they didn't understand His words. Then He said:

"One of you will betray Me. I will be arrested and killed."

The disciples were frightened and each of them asked, "Is it I?"

Judas also asked, "Am I the one?"

And he stretched out his hand to take a piece of bread.

The Lord knew that Judas had already betrayed Him but He did not tell His disciples. He only said:

"It is one of you who took the Bread from my hands."

But He had distributed the Bread to all of them! Only Judas understood that the Lord was speaking about him and so he immediately left and ran to the Pharisees to give them Christ.

The Lord Jesus Christ then began to speak to His disciples about everything that was most important that He had not told them before. He told them that He would soon leave them and that after that they would receive comfort and joy. Over and over again, He told them to love one another.

ARREST IN THE GARDEN OF GETHSEMANE

Night fell. Jesus Christ led all of His disciples into the Garden of Gethsemane and began to pray there.

He knew that very soon, people would come and seize Him.

And soon, they did come to get Him. There were soldiers and a crowd of many different people with torches and clubs. Judas said to the guards:

"The One that I kiss is Christ. Seize Him."

And so he approached the Lord Jesus Christ and called out: "Hail, teacher!"

He kissed Him.

Christ looked at him sadly and just said:

"Friend, why have you come?"

For He knew from the very beginning what Judas had come for.

Then he turned to the soldiers and said:

"I am the Man."

They were so afraid that they fell to the ground.

Then He said:

"If I wanted, a million angels would come to My aid. But do what you have come for. Only do not touch those who are with Me."

And so they seized Him.

THE CRUCIFIXION

When Christ was judged, they condemned Him to the worst punishment that there was: to be crucified on a Cross. He bore the terrible pain and wicked people mocked Him and said:

"You called Yourself the Son of God? You saved others and You cannot save Yourself? If you are the Son of God, come down from the Cross!"

He could have done that, but the reason why He had been born a Man was so that He could meet death and defeat it.

Two thieves were crucified with Him, one on either side. One of them also began to mock Christ to show everyone that he was brave and did not even fear pain or death:

"Hey, You, the Son of God! Come down from the cross. Save Yourself and us!"

But the other thief had pity on Christ and called out to his comrade:

"What is the matter with you? Do you have no conscience? Do you not fear God? We are being punished for the evil that we have done. But this Man has done nothing wrong!"

And he said to Jesus:

"Lord! Remember me when You come in Your Kingdom."

Jesus answered him:

"Today you will be with Me in Paradise!"

THE BURIAL OF CHRIST

Jesus Christ truly died on the Cross.

His most faithful friends and His mother, the Most-holy Theotokos, took His Body down from the Cross and buried it in a cave, just like Lazarus had been buried not long before.

His disciples were so overcome with grief that they never remembered that He had told them that He would rise from the dead. They thought they would never see Him again.

But the Pharisees who gave Him over to death heard and remembered that He had said, "I will rise from the dead," and they were afraid. What if His disciples came and took His body from the tomb and hid it and then told everyone that He had risen? Then people would believe in Him and no longer listen to them.

To make sure that did not happen, they put a seal on the large stone that had been placed in front of the tomb. If they tried to roll the stone away, the seal would be broken and everyone would see that someone had gone into the tomb. Then they put soldiers in front of the stone to guard the entrance into the tomb. At a distance stood the women who, like the disciples and Apostles, had followed Christ, listened to Him and loved and served Him. The soldiers did not let them get any closer, so they stood and wept.

HOW CHRIST BROKE
THE BONDS OF HADES

The first human beings that God created, Adam and Eve, lived in Paradise. But they were disobedient to God and so God drove them out of Paradise. Paradise was closed to mankind. When people died, they did not go to Paradise but to Hades. Both the righteous and the wicked went there. Those first human beings, Adam and Eve, were also there in the kingdom of darkness, where no one could see anyone else.

Then Christ God descended into Hades while His body was lying in the cave.

The gates of Hades were broken. It was as if lightning had illumined the darkness of Hades!

Christ took Adam and Eve by the hand and said:

"All who want to be with Me are free! Follow me! To Heaven!"

And so, all who wanted to, found themselves with God in Heaven, which we have not yet seen. There, where it is always bright, where God and Life reign, where there is only goodness and righteousness, all those who love one another meet and see each other in that light and love each other even more. That Kingdom of Light is called the Kingdom of Heaven.

WHAT HAPPENED THAT NIGHT
AT THE TOMB

The soldiers stood at the entrance of the cave, by the large stone that had been sealed. The stone was heavy. One person would not be able to move it without help. Night fell and the soldiers listened to hear if someone was coming.

Suddenly thunder rang out and the heavy stone rolled away from the tomb all by itself and an angel, shining like lightning, sat on the stone, dressed in clothes as white as snow.

The soldiers were afraid and fell to the ground as if they were dead and did not see or hear anything else.

When they came to themselves, they ran into the city, far away from the cave.

The Body of the Lord Jesus Christ was gone.

He had risen from the dead.

THE MORNING OF CHRIST'S RESURRECTION

Before the dawning of the sun, while it was still dark, the women who loved Christ came to the cave where He was buried. They wanted at least to care for His dead Body and so they brought myrrh with them, a fragrant oil that smelled like the best herbs and flowers, that smelled better than the most expensive perfume. That is why we call these women the Myrrh-bearing Women.

As they walked along the streets of the city in the darkness, they asked each other:

"Who will roll away the stone for us from the door of the tomb?"

They knew that they were not strong enough to roll away the stone. They knew that the tomb was guarded by soldiers. But they still hoped, because of how much they loved the Lord.

When they arrived, they saw that the stone had already been rolled away to the side and that the guards had fled. And in the tomb, there was no dead body to be found!

They did not understand what had happened...

Suddenly, an Angel in a shining robe appeared before them.

"Why are you seeking for the Living among the dead?" the angel asked. "He is not here. He is risen! Remember what He told you while He was still with you, that wicked men would seize Him and put Him to death and then He would rise from the dead!"

Only then did the Myrrh-bearing Women remember the words of the Lord Jesus, since they had also heard Him say that.

The Angel disappeared and the Myrrh-bearing Women ran to tell the disciples of Christ, the Apostles.

Later, the Apostles carried that news and the teaching of Christ throughout the whole world.

That is how the Church came into being.

WE ALSO WANT TO BE WITH
THE RISEN CHRIST

Christ is risen! Truly He is risen!

And that is why we can also rise from the dead and enter Paradise. We are Christians. We love Christ. And He loves us so much that He became a Man and even died so that He could raise us up with Himself and bring mankind with Him into Paradise. He wants us all to be as good as He is.

And if we try to be obedient and do what is right, then when we come to Church and receive Communion we will be even closer to God. Holy Communion is a sacred food that God has given to us just like Christ gave His disciples at the Mystical Supper. When we receive Communion, God's love fills us and helps us to become like Him.

OUR MOST IMPORTANT FEAST

We call the very best day of the week, Sunday, "the Day of Resurrection." Each week, we remember the Resurrection of Christ on Sunday. That is the day that people usually go to Church and many receive Communion. Sunday is always a feast!

But one Sunday each year is special – Pascha, the radiant feast of Christ's Resurrection. We spend more time getting ready for this feast than for any other. We dye eggs and decorate them, we bake kulich bread, and then we bring all of that to Church to be blessed. There, the priest will pray and then bless the things we bring with holy water. Then it will no longer be just tasty food, but food that is special, holy, and festive!

We do not just celebrate Pascha for one day only, but for a whole week – Bright Week! During the whole forty days after Pascha, we greet each other with the words, "Christ is risen!" and sing the Paschal troparion:

Christ is risen from the dead
Trampling down death by death
And upon those in the tombs
Bestowing life!

That means that Christ has conquered death and given the gift of eternal life to all those who have died.

During the Paschal season, we hear the words:

"Christ is risen!"

Then we answer:

"Truly He is risen!"

That means that the Resurrection of Christ is the most important truth and our chief joy in the whole world.

HOW TO TELL CHILDREN ABOUT
THE RESURRECTION OF CHRIST

The Resurrection of Christ is the center of our faith. Pascha is the most important feast for Orthodox Christians. The joy of Pascha permeates everything and even the littlest children can feel it. But it is not always easy to explain to a small child what happened and why the whole world is rejoicing.

Up to a certain age, nothing really needs to be explained. Children can feel the feast all around them and soak it in. But there comes an age when children begin to take an active role in learning and taking in the world around them and begin to ask questions about everything. We do not need to force that interest too early but we do need to be ready for it. This book will help support you when the moment comes.

The best time to start reading this book to your children is during Great Lent, when we are already looking forward to Pascha. If you read it for the first time a while before Pascha then it is a good idea to read it again during the days of Holy Week. Even before then, on Lazarus Saturday and Palm Sunday, it is good to read the chapters that correspond to those days. In any case, children are usually excited to read their favorite books over and over again and often ask for them. When you read the book for the first time to children between two and four years old, it is important to divide the reading up by chapters, reading one per day, or perhaps two if they are short. Then, you can tell your child that you will read the next chapter tomorrow. Of course, it is essential that you also take time to look over the pictures with them.

Your child might have questions about each part of the book and so we hope that the following chapter-by-chapter explanations and the glossary in the back will help you know how to answer.

GOD LOVES US ALL

In our series, "Scripture and Feasts for Children," there are two other books that also talk about the love of God – "The Miracles of Christ" and "The Nativity of Christ." Perhaps this little chapter might serve as a touchstone for how to talk to children about faith and answer whatever questions they might have. After all, it is essential that everything we tell children about Christ begin and end with the love God has for mankind. As much as you are willing and able, you can add your own personal experience and understanding to each sentence, expanding upon it, as you talk to your children.

This chapter briefly retells the story of the raising of Lazarus and just briefly mentions two other events from the Gospel: the raising of the son of the widow of Nain (Luke 7:11-16) and the raising of Jairus's daughter (Mark 5:22-24, 35-43; Luke 8:41-42, 49-56). If these stories catch your children's interest, you can read through the appropriate passages in the Gospel and then recount the stories to your children. You should retell them as simply as possible, conveying the essence of the story, trying to express the parts of the stories that touch our hearts and can, of course, touch the hearts of your children as well. Another book in this series, "The Miracles of Christ," has a chapter on the raising of the son of the widow of Nain.

If their development has not been burdened by tragedy and illness, children have a deep instinctive understanding of their own immortality during the first few years of life which only requires simple affirmation. People die but Christ has conquered death. "I will not die forever. I will rise!" is a truth that for children requires no "proof." Moreover, unnecessary attempts to explain and justify this truth to a child will only shake their conviction in the certainty of this truth, so it is not a good idea to burden a child with them.

But if, as your children grow, they begin to have questions about where death came from and what exactly it is, you should answer them. We would like to offer you an example of how to approach this discussion.

God made everything that exists. He created us, mankind, so that we would be like Him and always be good, always rejoice, always obey Him, and care for everything on earth – the animals, birds, fish, trees, and flowers. And He created us to love one another.

But once, a horrible tragedy happened. Instead of listening to God, people lied to Him. And after people were disobedient to God, they ceased being good and began to hurt each other and began to die. Death is mankind's most fearsome enemy (1 Corinthians 15:26).

Christ became Man so that He could conquer death. Christ rose from the dead and He will raise all those who love God and who want to be with Him for an unending life of joy.

THE ENTRANCE OF THE LORD INTO JERUSALEM
PALM SUNDAY

In former times, Palm Sunday was the main feast for children since it was children who greeted the Savior with especial joy as He entered into Jerusalem. This event from the Gospels is very dear to the hearts of children and easy for them to understand.

Lazarus Saturday and Palm Sunday are not part of Great Lent and so in traditionally Orthodox countries, these feasts used to be accompanied by public festivities and a bazaar. In Moscow, the bazaar took place on Red Square. It is wonderful if you are able to prepare your children for this radiant festival. You can take home the palm and pussy willow branches and you and your children can make little trees out of them or decorate them with colored ribbons, and paper angels and birds.

THE MYSTICAL SUPPER

"And that is how Jesus Christ for the first time gave Communion so that all who love Him could also receive Communion. Even today, He gives us Communion in His Body and Blood in Church so that, by receiving God, we can be united to Him."

Here we tell children about the Eucharist and about what it means. The first time you read this chapter, there is no reason to stop and give extended explanations but when you reread it, if you need to, you can talk more about Communion and show them not only the picture of the Mystical Supper but also the picture later on in the book of children receiving Communion in Church.

ARREST IN THE GARDEN OF GETHSEMANE, CRUCIFIXION, AND BURIAL

These chapters are the saddest and most difficult in the book. If your children are particularly impressionable and these chapters frighten them, you can help them by reminding them that Christ bore all of this in order to conquer death and rise from the dead. And he did conquer death. That is what this book is about. Be attentive and bright! Let the words of St. Seraphim of Sarov ring inside you as you read these chapters: "Christ is risen, my joy! We have no need to be cast down!"

The disciples of Christ did not remember that Christ would soon rise from the dead but we remember! We know! The Church of Christ lives by that knowledge.

At a certain moment, a child that may already be acquainted with the image of the Cross and the Crucifixion may suddenly realize that all of that is tied in with pain and suffering and feel a kind of confusion. Was it really painful for Him? They really pierced His hands with nails? How can that be? This happens with different children at different ages. Some children understand it surprisingly quickly while others only come to understand it gradually, over the course of years. But to answer all of the questions your children might have, both the ones they ask out loud and the ones they do not, point them to the Resurrection. Yes, He was in pain, He suffered for all people, in order to raise us from the dead like He rose, so that we can be with Him in the Kingdom of Heaven, where there is no pain or suffering.

HOW CHRIST BROKE THE BONDS OF HADES

This chapter of the book should be read separately. In essence, it is the central chapter of the whole book. The book's most important content is all contained here: heaven and hell, the first people, salvation, and the Kingdom of Heaven. All of that corresponds to what we see on the icon of the Descent into Hades, the icon of the Resurrection of Christ. Hopefully, the explanations given below for some difficult words will help you answer the questions your children might have.

If your children have still not heard the story of Adam and Eve, you might tell them their story in your own words as you read this chapter. A book in the series "Scripture and Feasts for Children" is planned that will talk about the first people in Paradise.

WHAT HAPPENED THAT NIGHT AT THE TOMB THE MORNING OF CHRIST'S RESURRECTION

The narrative in this book is focused primarily on the Resurrection of Christ as a fact of our own lives and less on the historical event meaning that we have left out some of the other historical events that took place after the resurrection, such as Christ appearing to Mary Magdalene and the Apostles. Christ rose from the dead, He freed those who were imprisoned in Hades, the grave was radiant with light, the guards lost consciousness, and a bright Angel proclaimed the resurrection to the Myrrh-bearing Women.

Later on, if your children express an interest in knowing "what it all was like," an interest that might be encouraged by Paschal songs or videos, you can read them excerpts from the four Gospels, especially the last chapter of each one. This works especially well during the days of Bright Week, but also throughout the whole Paschal season, all the way up to Ascension.

WE ALSO WANT TO BE WITH THE RISEN CHRIST

This chapter is a kind of outline for future discussions (God willing, more than one) with your children and a support for their entrance into the life of the Church. Communion, which is essential for our spiritual support and personal growth, is presented not as an obligation, but as a gift. We can draw near to Christ God. We can partake in His love. We can become like Him.

OUR MOST IMPORTANT FEAST

A book, of course, cannot ever be the main thing that draws a child into the atmosphere of the Feast. This book is only there to help. Getting ready for the Paschal feast in joyful anticipation, decorating eggs together, and most important of all, going to Church for the services, should not be things your child only reads about in a book.

Bring your children to Church on Holy Saturday morning. You can feel the feast drawing near! There are so many interesting things to see. On the eve of His Resurrection, the Savior is still resting in the flesh in the tomb but is already accomplishing what is depicted in the icon of the Descent to Hades. Bring them to Church with a basket of Paschal food to be blessed.

It takes children a long time to gain a precise sense of their relationship with time, to remember what "tomorrow" and "yesterday" are, what happened "long ago" and what will happen "soon." But that is a good thing because, as a result, their perception of Church feasts is in a way truer than our own. In the Church, the barrier between time and eternity is broken. In order for us, as adults, to understand that the events of the Gospels are not just historical events, but eternal realities, we may have to immerse ourselves in the works of great theologians and philosophers. But children understand. For them, the Gospels as an eternal reality is as obvious as "Christ is risen!" and that He will never again die. We must work carefully to preserve that divine "obviousness" for our children.

GLOSSARY

Pharisees - This word means "separated, special." These people thought of themselves as being righteous and teachers of the people, blindly following the Law. Christ condemned their false righteousness and spiritual blindness and the Pharisees hated Him.

Torch - A torch is a lantern made of a bundle of sticks with some flammable material at the end. A torch can burn for a long time and shines brightly in all sorts of weather. Before there were electric lights, streets were lit up at night by torches.

Paradise - Paradise is the abode of the angels and the righteous. It is the place where man can behold God and have communion with Him.

Apostles - These were the disciples of Christ that He sent to teach all people how to live according to the righteousness of God. The word "Apostle" means "one who is sent."

Hades - In Greek, this word means "a place without light," a place where sin is punished after death, where it is impossible to see and hear God.

Kingdom of Heaven - The Kingdom of Heaven is eternal life and blessedness in communion with God, where the Angels serve Him. The Kingdom of God itself comes to us on earth during the Liturgy. Liturgy teaches us to love all people. When we love each other, the Kingdom of God reigns in our hearts.

Holy Communion - By a divine miracle, the bread and wine that are brought to Liturgy become the Body and Blood of Jesus Christ. Although the Holy Gifts continue to look like bread and wine, when we taste them, we are united with the Risen Christ. He enters into our hearts and we receive immortality. Christ enters our hearts and we become citizens of the Kingdom of God.

CPSIA information can be obtained
at www.ICGtesting.com
Printed in the USA
LVHW011502060821
694670LV00005B/63

9 781950 067039